SWIFT SUCCESS GUIDES™

THE SMALL BUSINESS GROWTH BLUEPRINT

HOW TO GROW YOUR BUSINESS AND TURN CUSTOMERS INTO LIFELONG FANS

BRIDGET McCREA

STRONGTIDE PRESS

ISBN 979-8-9946587-0-3 (paperback)
ISBN 979-8-9946587-1-0 (ebook)

First Edition
Published by StrongTide Press
www.strongtidepress.com

Printed and distributed in the United States of America

This book is for informational and educational purposes only. The author is not an attorney, accountant or financial advisor. The book is not meant to provide legal, tax or financial advice. Laws, rules and requirements change. Every business situation is different, so please consult a qualified professional for guidance specific to you.

Any products, services, URLs or organizations mentioned are included for reference only. The author has no affiliation, endorsement or agreements with them. Use your own judgment before acting on any information provided in the following pages.

Contents

INTRODUCTION:
KEEP CUSTOMERS SO HAPPY
THEY NEVER LEAVE

If there was a way to keep your customers so happy that they just kept coming back to your business again and again, you'd want to know the secret, right? It would mean that even with your closest competitor being one click or tap away, that buyer would just keep coming back for more. If this sounds like a dream world, think again. Despite the high competition for every eyeball, click and buy, there are still ways to stand out in this noisy world and retain clients for life.

Unfortunately, there's no silver bullet that applies to every business, so I'll start by sharing my own experience, knowing that not every business owner will relate to it. Still, it helps illustrate the point, so bear with me. Anyone who was around for the early days of the commercial internet probably remembers what America Online (AOL) was like before the whole platform got weird and eventually disappeared. At the time, it was a freelance writer's dream. It gave us a new way to connect with editors and clients without typing up query letters and schlepping down to the post office and anxiously waiting weeks for a response.

Anyway, when I saw that the editor of *Industrial Distribution* was looking for writers on AOL, I responded. I was working for a welding distributor in Pennsylvania and saw it as a possible entryway into writing for B2B publications (known as "trade magazines" at that time). We connected, I got my first assignment and then got to work. After that first article was accepted and published, I went on to write many of *Industrial Distribution's* sponsored content and advertorials.

If you know anything about the publishing industry, you know it's a dynamic sector where magazines and other publications tend to change hands a lot. Publishers consolidate, acquire new titles, fold non-performing ones and sometimes go out of business altogether. *Industrial Distribution* was purchased by Reed Business Information along with sister publications *Logistics Management* and *Modern Materials Handling*, both of which are now owned by Peerless Media.

With all of that change happening around the industry, one thing didn't change: I still have the same client I started with back in 1994. My original editor has long since retired, but through ownership changes, economic swings and shifts in how content gets produced, I've not only maintained the relationship but expanded it into new opportunities. For example, when Peerless Media branched out into sponsored marketing content, they called on me to contribute outside of traditional editorial. It was a great opportunity, and one I gratefully accepted and continue to enjoy.

Most of my other clients have come and gone over the last 25+ years, and that's pretty normal in my line of work. Freelancers are freelancers for a reason. We enjoy diving into different topics, formats and opportunities. We don't like being tied to a single employer, and we've learned how to ebb and flow with a marketplace that never stands still. But like everyone else, we also value some level of certainty and steady work that pays the bills. That's where the idea of "clients for life" comes into the picture.

7 Reasons Some Customer Relationships Last

After writing *Your First Business Blueprint,* a book that helps new entrepreneurs launch their companies, and *Blueprints Beat Cocktail*

Napkins, which gives them a usable way to think through business planning, I noticed a clear pattern. Businesses weren't failing because they lacked ideas or ambition; they were struggling because once they got past the starting line, they didn't have systems in place to hold onto the customers they worked so hard to win.

So, what does it take to keep a client for life, not just through one project or one good stretch, but across ownership changes, economic swings and shifts you don't control? Looking back, it wasn't one big decision. It was a series of smaller ones, made again and again, often even when it was inconvenient. Here's what I've found works best:

> **#1) Always put them first, even when you're busy.** Most business relationships don't end because of a single dramatic event. Instead, they taper off when customers start to feel like a transaction instead of a priority. That shows up everywhere and I've had it happen many times in my own business, even if I hate to admit it. A food truck regular who waits longer than usual and gets brushed aside. An Etsy buyer whose order shows up late and doesn't come back the next time they need a gift. The auto detailing client that found a better deal and experience elsewhere. Nothing was technically "wrong," but the experience just wasn't the same for those customers. The businesses that keep customers long-term notice those moments and course-correct before they snowball into real problems. Customers don't expect to be your only focus, but they do want to know that they matter when it's their turn and when they don't, they move on.

#2) Say yes when new opportunities surface. Long-time clients need to know you're in it for the long haul. When they veer off in a new direction, you're right there figuring out how you fit into it and support their mission. The same goes when things tighten up. Budgets get cut. Projects pause. Work slows down for reasons that have nothing to do with you. Clients notice when you vanish the minute the situation isn't ideal. If you stay engaged, adjust expectations and ride out the dip with them, they notice that too. This how you become the indispensable "go to" provider.

#3 Stay present even when under scrutiny. Clients don't send out a memo announcing they're reassessing vendors. They just start paying closer attention: Who's being responsive? Who's thinking ahead? Who's still engaged when the work gets unpredictable? Many customer relationships don't end with a complaint or a refund. They fade when follow-up stops, and your attention shifts to other priorities.

#4 Get client management systems in place early. Nothing erodes goodwill faster than making a customer feel like they have to start from scratch every time they talk to you. Repeating back stories, explaining preferences over and over again, and highlighting recurring issues is just exhausting. Businesses that keep customers long-term pay attention. They remember how someone likes to work and can quickly reference past projects without digging through old emails and notes. Putting good customer management systems in early (it can be as basic as a simple, inexpensive cloud-based CRM), pays off over time.

#5) Make the relationship about them, not you. Strong retention shows up in routine moments, not big initiatives. Following up, closing loops and responding without always trying to sell something signal that the relationship still matters. When those signals disappear, customers start looking for new providers. You can minimize the churn by putting them at the center of everything you do.

#6) Treat your customer's customers like they matter. Missed emails, sloppy communication and avoidable problems don't just affect you, they also affect your client's reputation. The vendors that last understand this and act accordingly. They respond promptly and stay professional, and don't create messes their client has to clean up later. Helping them look good to their own customers isn't always easy, but it's definitely one of the fastest ways to show that you're truly part of the team.

#7) Never lower the bar just because you're busy. One of the fastest ways businesses lose customers is by letting standards slip when things get hectic. Calls get shorter; follow-up turns into an afterthought; and the small touches that made the experience feel solid start fading away. Businesses that keep customers long-term decide early on what "good" looks like and refuse to let that erode, even when they're stretched thin. Remember: consistency matters more than effort and when the basics start to slip, your customers notice (and don't always talk to you about it).

Businesses that keep customers also avoid tricks and shortcuts. Instead, they pay attention, show up the same way over time and prove themselves to be reliable, especially amid changing conditions. They don't treat relationships like something that resets every time the work shifts, the economy dips or a disruptive event throws things out of whack. That combination of steadiness and reliability keeps customers coming back long after the novelty wears off.

Making the Case for Delighted Customers

Before diving into tactics and real-world examples of companies that get this right, let's step back and look at why customers for life matter as much as they do.

The reality is that things change faster than ever. We all have more choices, more access and more ways to buy than any generation before us, largely due to the internet but there are some other forces at work here. In nearly every situation, your nearest competitor is one tap or click away.

This fundamentally changed how customers think about loyalty. Rewind the clock and the picture looks very different. Most of our grandparents probably shopped at the same neighborhood grocery store and took their car to the same local mechanic, not because they were making a conscious loyalty choice, but because there weren't many alternatives. The same was often true for our parents, who may have bought the same brands they saw on television and went to the same restaurants year after year for similar reasons. Options were limited, switching took effort and loyalty was often built into the system.

That world is gone and today's customers—and the companies they do business with—operate in a very different reality made up of:

- **Customers who can compare and switch almost instantly, which changes how buying decisions get made.** Prices, reviews and alternatives sit a few taps away, so customers rarely feel locked in. When something feels slow, confusing or off, they don't overthink it. They just shop around.

- **Switching that's easy, cheap and low lift.** Changing brands, providers or platforms doesn't take much effort. Accounts transfer easily, subscriptions cancel quickly, and competitors work hard to make onboarding painless. Convenience no longer protects loyalty.

- **Choice that raises expectations across the board.** Price still matters, but so do responsiveness and consistency. What once counted as strong service now feels like the baseline, and anything less stands out immediately.

- **Constant disruption, with new competitors, platforms and business models appearing all the time.** Customers don't wait for markets to settle or for businesses to catch up. They adapt quickly and move on just as quickly. Keeping up with them is difficult, but not impossible.

- **Loyalty that must be earned repeatedly. Habit and convenience no longer carry the weight they once did.** Customers stay because a business delivers reliability, attention and follow-through long after the first sale.

As you can see, it's not habit or convenience that creates lifetime customers. Those unbreakable ties are built on consistency, reliability, attention and delighted customers who have a reason to stay. Next, let's look at why this matters and what happens when businesses ignore it.

Why Churn Rates Matter

The numbers around customer retention don't leave much room for debate. Numerous studies reveal just how expensive it is to win a new customer than keep an existing one. Researchers have measured this gap across sectors and the difference shows up consistently. Here's the main reason why:

> *Every time a customer leaves, a company has to spend more money on marketing, sales, onboarding and trust-building just to get back to where it started. Over time, that cycle drains resources, impedes growth and throttles profitability.*

Repeat that short phrase back to yourself a few times and it starts to make sense, right? After all, every lost customer puts you right back at the starting line, spending time and money just to replace something you already had at some point. Also, the clients who stay don't need to be convinced to buy your products or services again. They already know you, trust you and chose you once.

Some of the more widely-reported customer acquisition statistics say it takes anywhere from five to 25 times more money to acquire a new client rather than keep an existing one, one *HBR* article reports. Bain and Co., also says that when you increase customer retention rates by just 5%, your company's profits may increase anywhere from 25% to 95%. These statistics haven't been updated recently, but I'm guessing both are higher now based on the rapid changes we've seen in both the selling environment and the world in general.

The *HBR* article goes on to explain the importance of customer retention and how to use churn rate to track the percentage of clients who leave during a specific period of time. Companies measure churn rate differently based on what they sell, but in all cases the ones that keep their customers prioritize retention and bake it into their operations.

Spot Customer Churn Before it Starts

Companies that keep their customers don't wait for churn to become a problem. They think about it early and often, and usually before the first deal closes. Even if you don't have paying customers yet, this quick gut check will help you spot gaps that drive people away.

Quick Customer Churn Gut Check

→ **Do customers know what to expect after buying from you?** Uncertainty creates extra steps and hassle fast. When customers don't know what happens next, confidence drops and the urge to come back fades.

→ **What happens after the transaction is done?** If the relationship goes silent the moment money changes hands, don't be surprised when customers start to drop off.

→ **Do customers know how to reach you if something goes wrong?** If they have to hunt for answers, frustration sets in fast.

→ **Do problems get resolved quickly and clearly?** Issues are going to surface, but customers remember how long they wait for an answer and whether they had to chase you down for it.

→ **Do returning customers feel recognized?** Repeat customers shouldn't feel like strangers every time they come back. Recognition builds continuity, and continuity builds trust.

→ **Do you know which customers haven't come back lately?** Customer loss usually happens gradually. If you aren't tracking who stopped coming back, you'll miss the early signals and the chance to course correct.

If you answered "no" to one or more of these questions, it's time to take a closer look at what happens after the sale, before those gaps start costing your customers.

So what does it really take to lower churn and keep customers for life? This book covers that topic in depth, but let's start by pulling some tips from Salesforce's 360 Blog. After stripping away the marketing gloss, it comes down to a short list of behaviors that consistently show up in companies with strong retention:

➤ **Get the first experience right.** The old adage about never getting another chance to make a first impression applies here. Customers decide early whether they're coming back. Clear onboarding, simple next steps and no question as to what happens after the first purchase all count here.

➤ **Respond fast when something breaks.** Customers don't expect perfection, but they do expect a fast response. Slow replies, unanswered questions and vague follow-ups are common reasons people move on (and what drives negative reviews).

➤ **Treat repeat customers differently.** As you read in my own personal story in this chapter, returning customers already trust you. They shouldn't feel like they're starting from scratch every time. Recognition, continuity and familiarity go a long way.

➤ **Make it easy to buy again.** This is an important one because retention improves when repeat purchases require less effort than the first one. Focus on fewer steps and an easier path to "yes" the second time around.

➤ **Pay attention to who comes back.** Businesses that track repeat customers tend to spot churn earlier. You'll miss the warning signs if you're only tracking new leads.

➤ **Build consistency into everyday interactions.** Strong retention doesn't come from one big moment. It comes from doing the basics well, over and over again, even when things get hectic and you're being pulled in 10 different directions.

Salesforce also reinforces a broader point that's covered in a lot of studies, and that's that repeat customers drive a <u>disproportionate share</u> of small business revenue and create more predictable growth for those companies. Sales volume gets the attention, but predictability pays the bills whether you're running a corner shop or a Fortune 500 organization.

What You'll Learn In This Book

This chapter laid the groundwork for everything that follows by showing how customer relationships are built or lost long before churn ever shows up on a report. You learned that customers don't leave because of one giant mistake. More often than not, the drivers are missed signals, fading attention and small breakdowns that go unaddressed. The examples here (including my own) all point to the same conclusion: long-term customer relationships come from consistent behavior over time, not clever tactics or one-time wins.

This book will help you see who your best customers really are, how buying behavior has shifted and where you're losing people without realizing it. Keeping customers isn't about grand gestures or one-time fixes. It's about what you do every day. So the advice here is practical, grounded and built for actual use. If you're trying to build or grow a business and need to hold on to the customers you work so hard to win, keep reading.

Put This Chapter to Work By:

☞ **Writing down what happens after someone buys from you.** Include confirmation, follow-up and how problems get handled so customers never fall into a black hole.

☞ **Picking one customer you don't want to lose.** Watch how the relationship actually works. How often do you check in? How fast do you respond? Do they have to chase you down?

☞ **Choosing a single, basic standard and sticking to it.** Decide how fast you'll respond or follow up and don't let that slide (even when things get busy).

☞ **Using the churn gut check as a starting point.** Any question you answer "no" to may already be a point where customers may be considering your competitors.

 **Make This Your Next Step**
Fix one small point of confusion or delay in your post-purchase process this week, even if it feels minor.

STAGE 1

EARN THE RELATIONSHIP

1

KNOW YOUR CUSTOMER

If you're starting or growing a business, your instinct is probably to get as many customers as you can. That's natural. You need traction and revenue, and a packed pipeline looks and feels like success. Your CRM is getting populated, the orders are going out and people are buying what you're selling.

Unfortunately, taking on just any client isn't a good path to keeping customers for life. Sure there are some businesses that thrive on one-off sales, but even an e-commerce seller with minimal direct customer interactions (e.g., a company selling mostly through Amazon) would want "raving fans" that come back when it's time to buy more, upgrade or try something new. This applies where we're talking about a restaurant owner, an indie book publisher, a boutique accounting firm or an Etsy seller.

Knowing your customer doesn't mean trying to understand everyone who might buy from you. It means knowing who you can serve well, keep happy and continue working with. That way, instead of chasing every opportunity that walks through the door, you can focus on what actually builds a business: customers who stick around.

Here's What Happens When You Chase Every Customer

Trying to be everything to everyone usually starts with good intentions, especially in the startup stage or during a growth push, but it's not sustainable. In fact, it spreads your time, attention and energy too thin instead of creating momentum. This makes it harder to deliver a consistent experience. The work also gets harder to manage, decisions take longer and customers start to pick up an underlying problem.

Here are 10 telltale signs that it's time to tighten up your customer description and retention efforts:

1. You're explaining the same basics over and over again instead of getting work done, because customers come in with very different expectations.

2. Pricing takes longer to explain and defend, because what feels fair to one customer feels too high or confusing to the next.

3. Service feels inconsistent because your processes don't gel well with everyone you've decided to work with or sell to.

4. Some customers never seem satisfied because they just weren't a good match in the first place.

5. You spend more time putting out small fires because each customer wants things handled a little differently.

6. Follow-up starts slipping, not from neglect but because too many clients are competing for your attention.

7. Your best customers get less of your time, even though they're the ones most likely to stay, refer others and stick with you for life.

8. Your message gets fuzzy, making it harder for new customers to quickly understand what you actually do.

9. Simple decisions start to feel harder because every choice seems to disappoint someone.

10. Customers leave because they never really fit with your organization and its products/service (and never fully settled into using them).

If one or more of these signs is relatable, it's a reminder that you don't have to <u>serve everyone</u> to build a strong, successful business. When you focus on the customers who fit how you actually work, everything from day-to-day decisions to long-term relationships gets easier to manage.

Your Customers Need Guidance, Not More Choices

Today's customers have more choices, more noise competing for their attention and fewer reasons to stick around. This has led to:

→ **Ease of switching brands.** One click and it's done.

→ **Availability of alternatives.** There's always another option right in front of them.

→ **Short attention spans.** It's harder to hold attention past the first interaction.

→ **Customer expectations.** They change frequently and keeping up with them can be difficult.

→ **Comparison shopping.** Customers keep comparing, even long after they buy.

→ **Lack of loyalty.** It just doesn't stick the way it used to.

→ **Over-communication.** Let's face it, most messages get ignored.

→ **Poor follow-up.** One follow-up often isn't enough, yet that's usually about all a business is ready to give.

→ **Reputation matters less.** And finally, being "known" doesn't carry as much weight anymore.

The challenges don't end there. The price of landing a customer (also known as customer acquisition cost or CAC) climbs every year, and especially for companies operating in the real estate, financial services, legal services, manufacturing and higher education sectors. Some of the lower CAC industries include B2B software as a service (SaaS), entertainment, construction, IT services and commercial insurance.

While CAC varies by industry, retention costs are generally five to 25 times lower than acquisition costs across all sectors. Meaning, it's a lot cheaper to keep a current customer happy than it is to find new ones.

Here are some other good reasons smart companies focus on retention over acquisition:

> Long-term customers tend to spend more money with your company over time, making them especially critical to sustainable growth.

> By one research firm's estimates, improving your customer retention rates by just 5% can boost profits by 25% to 95%. The theory being that repeat customers 1) tend to spend more over time, and 2) are less expensive to maintain.

> The likelihood of successfully selling to an existing customer is approximately 60-70%, but that figure drops to just 5-20% for a new one.

> Loyal buyers spend more money and adopt new products and services faster than new customers do.

> Return buyers are also 50% more likely to test out a new product or service. And, they spend just over 30% more on average compared to new clients.

Numbers and statistics aside, retention is worth your time because it builds on effort you've already put in. That's right, you already did the hard part. You found the lead, earned the trust, closed the sale and delivered. When that customer comes back, you're not starting from zero; you're extending the value of work you've already paid for (instead of scrambling to replace it with a new buyer).

Of course, this isn't about ignoring new customers. You'll ideally always have fresh business coming in, new prospects to add to your pipeline and new customer segments to explore. However, when every sale feels like it has to start from scratch, the pressure adds up fast. Retention takes some of that weight off by creating momentum that doesn't have to be recreated over and over again.

Walmart & Target Stay in Their Lanes

Sorry Hard Rock Café, but with few very exceptions the "love all, serve all" strategy doesn't work well in business. Even giant retailers like Walmart and Target make clear choices about price, experience and service, then live with the tradeoffs. They stay in their respective lanes and focus on their core customer bases.

For shoppers like me, the Walmart vs. Target decision sometimes comes down to which store is closer and whether one of them forces a left turn across traffic on the way home. For the companies and their shareholders, though, the differences between the two retailers run much deeper.

Walmart customers tend to:

* Skew older, with a strong concentration among Baby Boomers and older Gen X shoppers.

* Fall into middle-income households, commonly in the roughly $40,000–$80,000 annual income range.

* Live in suburban, small-town or rural areas where Walmart often serves as a primary retailer.

* Shop frequently for everyday necessities, treating Walmart as a routine stop rather than a discretionary one.

While Target customers:

* Skew younger, with a heavy concentration of Millennials and Gen X shoppers, especially ages 18–44.

* Earn higher household incomes on average, often around $80,000, with a meaningful share above $100,000.

* Live primarily in suburban areas, often in households with children.

* Shop less frequently but more intentionally, often for apparel, home goods or seasonal purchases.

To the naked eye, these two retailers are competing for the same shoppers. In reality, they serve diverse buyers with different habits, expectations and reasons for coming back again and again. Each company knows who it's serving, makes clear choices with that customer in mind and accepts the tradeoffs that come with those choices (i.e., Target leaves some discount-driven shoppers on the table while Walmart focuses on customers who are buying everyday essentials). That focus allows both to earn repeat business at massive scale without trying to please everyone.

Small business can borrow a page from these large retailers' playbooks. You don't need Walmart's reach or Target's branding to win customers for life, but must decide who your business is really built for. Then, use that profile to shape your pricing, service and follow-up strategies. When your business aligns with the customers who are the best fit for it, loyalty becomes much easier to earn and harder to lose.

It's Never Too Late to Get to Know Your Ideal Customer

Here's a quiz to help you see whether the customers you're attracting match how your business actually runs and where repeat business is most likely to come from. Read each statement and answer yes, sometimes or no based on how things work in your business right now (not how you'd like them to work). Circle your answers here or jot them down in a notebook:

I can clearly describe my ideal customer without listing every type of customer I've ever had.

Yes   Sometimes   No

Most of my customers understand what I sell before I have to explain it in detail.

Yes   Sometimes   No

My pricing makes sense to the majority of my customers without long justifications.

Yes   Sometimes   No

The customers I enjoy working with tend to stick around or come back.

Yes   Sometimes   No

I know which customers are most likely to refer others to my business.

Yes   Sometimes   No

I can point to at least one type of customer I chose not to pursue.

Yes   Sometimes   No

My marketing attracts customers who fit how my business actually operates.

Yes   Sometimes   No

I rarely feel pressured to change my processes just to close a sale.

Yes   Sometimes   No

I can describe what success looks like for my ideal customer after they buy from me.

Yes   Sometimes   No

When I think about growing my business, I envision more of the same kinds of customers that I'm already serving or working with.

Yes   Sometimes   No

Now, tally your score and see which category you land in:

Mostly "Yes" answers mean you have a solid handle on who you're serving, even if there's room to tighten things up.

A mix of "Yes" and "Sometimes" suggests you're on the right track but may be sending mixed signals to the market.

A lot of "No" answers usually means your customer base has grown without much direction, which is fairly common and fixable.

If your answers leaned heavily toward "Sometimes" or "No," it usually means your business grew faster than your customer definition did. The good news is that this book will help you tighten that focus and get on track now.

As a writer, my goal is always to offer advice you can actually use. Based on your answers to the quiz, here are some steps you can take now:

→ **Study the customers who stay.** Look at your repeat customers and long-term clients and ask what they have in common, not just demographically but also in how they work with you.

→ **Name who you're <u>not</u> for.** Write down one or two types of customers you'll stop chasing, even if they still show up occasionally. This simple action can improve retention.

→ **Simplify your message.** Adjust your website, socials or sales conversations so they speak directly to your best-fit customers instead of trying to cover every possible use case.

→ **Align your process with your customer.** Make sure your selling, delivery and follow-up approaches match your ideal customer's expectations (not just what a one-one customer asked for).

→ **Make your next hire, offer or marketing campaign customer-specific.** Before you make a serious change, question whether it will attract more of the customers you want to keep.

One more thing: you can't just create a picture of your ideal customer and use it forever. In fact you, should do it at least annually and anytime you:

- Launch a new product or service
- Raise or change your pricing structure
- Find yourself operating in a changing or disruptive market
- Start to notice that your best customers "look different"
- Feel like sales are getting more difficult to close

You don't have to rewrite your playbook and toss your current customer list every time one of these things happens, but you should consider small, intentional adjustments as your business matures. This will help you sharpen your decisions, focus on what's important and create clear messaging that resonates with your target audience. Get this part right and you won't just be building a pipeline. You'll be building customers for life.

Put This Chapter to Work By:

☞ **Documenting what happens after your next sale.** Write down when customers hear from you again and who handles that follow-up.

☞ **Identifying one point where customers tend to drop off.** Look for gaps after delivery, onboarding or between repeat purchases.

☞ **Listing the digital tools you already use to manage customers.** Include email, scheduling, CRM, invoicing or project tools and note what each one supports.

☞ **Auditing which retention tasks are automated versus manual.** Flag the areas where a simple trigger, template or reminder could prevent drop-off.

Make This Your Next Step
Choose one digital tool you already have and use it to automate a single post-sale follow-up this week.

2

DIGITAL OPENED DOORS, NOT SHORTCUTS

Want to know what really transformed the relationship between businesses and customers? It was digital. Not all at once, and not always in obvious ways, but steadily and permanently. That shift shapes how businesses connect, compete and grow today.

Now digital didn't arrive with a countdown clock, a clear starting line or really much of a warning to be honest. We all knew it was there, lingering in the background at first and then creeping in via small, practical moves: a website here, an email address on a business card, a customer who casually said, "Oh, we already looked you up online."

As a business journalist covering the shift in real time, I watched companies debate whether digital was something to experiment with or something they could afford to ignore a little longer. Social took a similar trajectory, eventually becoming the most visible and influential piece of digital marketing for many businesses.

Digital Broke Down Barriers

Before digital, marketing came with built-in limits. Geography, location, printing costs and distribution all mattered. Businesses usually found customers by showing up in person, building relationships and earning attention over time. The needle didn't move as quickly as it does in the digital world, but it did follow a steady and familiar path.

Then those limits started to fall away. And while the dot-com bomb of 2000–2002 impeded some of its progress, digital's siren's song proved too hard to ignore. There was a pause as investors licked their wounds and reassessed the money they were funneling into dot-coms, but customers were already hooked. Modern e-commerce channels didn't even exist yet, but buyers kept searching online, comparing options and getting comfortable with a faster, more transparent way to buy products and services.

For proof, we can look back at some of the companies that <u>didn't</u> survive the evolution.

Once a permanent fixture on kitchen counters and office desks nationwide, the Yellow Pages stopped being the default place people looked when they needed a plumber, a lawyer or a contractor. People searched online instead. Encyclopedia Britannica and companies like it followed a similar path to obscurity. These thick books packed with knowledge carried authority, history and credibility, but none of that mattered once information became searchable, clickable and constantly updated online.

Retail and media weren't far behind. Blockbuster didn't collapse because it wasn't watching the trends. It went out of business because customers stopped driving to its stores to browse shelves, pick out movies and the pay late fees when they weren't returned on time. Streaming removed that resistance and voila, no more Blockbuster. And Kodak didn't lack digital technology, but the company hit a wall when digital photography changed how people took photos, how often they took them and how quickly they shared them. All this undercut an age-old business model that Kodak was built on.

The list of companies that failed to keep up, and that aren't around anymore, goes on. But even as digital opened doors that hadn't existed before, it didn't offer shortcuts once customers walked through those doors. Sure visibility became easier, the world flattened out a bit and a global audience was suddenly within reach, but none of that guaranteed customer trust, loyalty or repeat business. And while it leveled the playing field for new entrants, digital also made it much harder to stand out from the clutter and keep customers on the hook for multiples sales and engagements.

Quick Retention Signal Check

Businesses that keep customers long-term don't nail everything every time. What they do get right is the basics, consistently. Customers notice that familiarity and stick with it. Here's a quick retention signal check you can use to gauge your own business. Read through the signals below and note those that are consistently true for your business:

After the First Sale

Check the signals:

☐ Customers don't have to ask what happens next
☐ Timing and communication expectations are clear
☐ The handoff from sale to delivery or service feels seamless

Follow-Up and Continuity

Check the signals:
☐ Follow-up continues after delivery, not just until the transaction closes

☐ Customers hear from us even when nothing's wrong
☐ Communication stays visible between transactions

Repeat Customer Experience

Check the signals:

☐ You can quickly recognize returning customers
☐ Past decisions and history don't need to be repeated
☐ Buying again feels familiar and efficient

Responsiveness and Trust

Check the signals:

☐ Customers know how to reach us and when to expect a response
☐ Questions and issues get resolved without repeated nudging
☐ Small problems don't turn into long delays

Visibility and Awareness

Check the signals:

☐ We can see which customers return and when
☐ We notice when regular customers stop coming back
☐ Repeat business happens by design, not by accident

Consistency

Check the signals:

- [ ] The experience matches what was promised
- [ ] Service quality stays steady regardless of timing or workload
- [ ] Customer information is tracked and accessible (and not just stored in someone's head)

If most of these signals felt familiar, that's a good sign. Customers don't come back by accident. They return because the experience feels familiar, predictable and easy to repeat. Now if a few areas stood out as weak, that's where repeat business breaks down and retention gets challenging.

The good news is that you can fix the problem. Start by looking at what happens after the sale closes. Customers should know when they'll hear from you again and who to contact if questions come up. Then, look at what happens after delivery. Many businesses fade into the background at this moment as they move onto the new project, sale or task. Even one planned follow-up post-sale can help nurture the relationship and make it easier for customers to return.

Finally, focus on continuity. Repeat business breaks down when customers have to start from scratch every single time. Try keeping basic customer histories accessible and refer to them as new orders or inquiries come in. When it's easy to pick up where things left off, customers are less likely to look elsewhere.

From Enterprise-Only to Everyday Use

Most of this chapter focuses on the impact of digital on the broader customer relationship, a real and relevant issue for every business operating today. Digital flattened the world and increased competition, but it also put better tools within reach. We have systems that help manage customer information, tools that support follow-up and communication and applications that make it easier to stay in touch after the sale.

Add in email platforms, scheduling tools and basic CRM software, and these options are affordable and accessible for businesses of all sizes. Even enterprise resource planning (ERP) platforms, which were once reserved for very large organizations, are now available via subscription and in scaled-down versions that cater to smaller firms.

That shift didn't happen overnight. The democratization of these tools unfolded gradually, with cloud computing doing much of the heavy lifting. It moved software from something businesses had to buy, install and maintain to something they could access on-demand in the cloud. There was a time when Marketo and Eloqua were two of the few serious options for automating marketing tasks at scale, and their price tags put them out of reach for most small businesses. Today, that same category includes simpler, lower-cost tools that let businesses start small and add capabilities over time.

Digital didn't change what keeps customers coming back, but it made the work behind it easier to organize, track and repeat. Whether you automate a little or a lot, focus on making follow-up routine, keeping past customer details handy and staying in touch after the sale. Those steps create retention better than any technology platform ever will.

20 Ways Digital Earns Its Keep

The digital world doesn't just make things harder. It also gives businesses real advantages they couldn't get before. Some require a budget or outside help, like web design, social marketing or search engine optimization (SEO). Others are free to anyone willing to figure them out. Here are 20 different ways you can leverage digital as a customer retention tool:

1. **Spell out what happens next after the sale.** Use order confirmations, onboarding emails or calendar invites to explain timing, next steps and who to contact. Customers shouldn't have to guess.

2. **Schedule one post-delivery check-in.** Set a follow-up email, task reminder or calendar alert to check in after the work is done. This keeps the relationship active once payment clears.

3. **Make it easy for customers to reach you again.** Create a clear contact page, use emails customers can reply to and monitor the inbox so they don't hit dead ends.

4. **Keep past customer details handy.** Store notes on prior work, preferences and timing in a simple CRM, shared document or project system so context is always available.

5. **Recognize returning customers quickly.** Use order history, tags or notes to acknowledge past work instead of starting from scratch.

6. **Stay "lightly" visible between transactions.** Send an occasional email update or post a brief update on your socials so customers don't lose track of you.

7. **Ask for reviews while goodwill is high.** Send review requests through email or text shortly after a positive experience, not months later.

8. **Centralize incoming communication.** Route emails, contact forms and messages into one shared inbox so you never miss one.

9. **Set clear response-time expectations.** Use auto-replies or helpdesk messages to let customers know when they'll hear back.

10. **Replace memory with reminders.** Use task lists, calendar alerts or project checklists instead of mental notes.

11. **Track repeat visits and purchases.** Review website traffic, order history or booking data to see who comes back and how often.

12. **Watch for drop-off signals early.** Notice when regular customers stop opening emails, booking appointments or visiting your site.

13. **Standardize common responses.** Create email templates or saved replies to keep information consistent and accurate.

14. **Make repeat purchases easy.** Offer rebooking links, saved forms or quick reorder options so customers don't have to re-enter information.

15. **Maintain service quality during busy periods.** Use digital checklists or workflows to keep standards steady when demand spikes.

16. **Store customer files in shared cloud folders.** Keep documents, images or records accessible so work doesn't stall when someone's on vacation or out sick.

17. **Group customers in simple ways.** Sort customers by what they buy, when they buy it or how often they're back. The will help you follow up without making it more complicated than it needs to be.

18. **Use social channels to respond, not broadcast.** Reply to comments and messages promptly instead of focusing on the number of posts you do per week or month.

19. **Test small changes fast.** Try different email timing, tweak your messaging or shift when you follow up. You don't need to rebuild the whole system to see what works.

20. **Stick to the basics and use them consistently.** Email platforms, scheduling software, shared records and simple analytics help you stay on top of follow-up and keep the relationship going.

Their Blind Spot is Your Opportunity

Digital made it easier to launch, easier to compete and way easier for customers to move on. But it didn't eliminate the advantage that comes from paying attention. CustomerGauge research shows that less than half of all B2B companies even measure customer retention. Not everyone reading this runs a B2B business, but the point stands: most companies still don't know who's coming back, who's leaving or why. That's your opening to do better.

Here are some real-world examples of this in action, from CustomerGauge:

- ☑ **Heineken** treats retention as relationship-building, not damage control. Leadership focuses on asking better questions consistently and using feedback to strengthen long-term customer ties, not just close the next sale.

- ☑ **Sweet Fish Media** reduced customer churn by first admitting it had no system for tracking it. After restructuring that system and introducing regular customer reviews, the company cut monthly churn dramatically in less than a year.

- ☑ **SugarCRM** made retention part of every strategic decision by constantly asking whether an action helped create a customer for life. Regular feedback loops and visible follow-through built trust and kept customers engaged across the entire organization.

- ☑ **HeidelbergCement** strengthened retention by following up personally with customers who raised concerns. Local teams acted on feedback quickly, which improved response rates and reinforced long-term relationships.

All of these companies operate in different industries, but the lesson here is the same: businesses that measure retention, listen after the sale and act on what they learn gain an advantage many of their competitors miss out on. The door is wide open, and this is your chance to turn routine transactions into repeat business. At minimum you should track repeat activity, check in after the sale, ask a couple of consistent questions and then act on the answers.

Use digital systems to support the process. That way, follow-up happens even when you are busy and nothing slips through the cracks. Most businesses still don't do this consistently, so the bar is lower than you think. While competitors are out there chasing new leads, you're building loyalty, predictable revenue and a business that sustains itself.

———————

If this chapter helped you rethink how digital affects customer retention or clarified where your follow-up needs work, a short Amazon review helps other business owners decide whether this book is right for them. Even a few words helps. Thanks for taking a moment to share your experience.

Put This Chapter to Work By:

☞ **Writing down who your business is and isn't built for.** Be specific enough that you'd feel comfortable saying "no" to a prospect without questioning your decision.

☞ **Envisioning your first five customers.** Focus on how they buy, what they value and why you're setting your sights on them.

☞ **Checking whether your pricing makes sense for the customers you want of.** If you're constantly explaining or defending it, something's off.

☞ **Reading your own marketing materials like you're seeing them for the first time.** Does the content speak to your ideal customer, or is it trying to be everything to everyone?

Make This Your Next Step
Describe your ideal first customer in writing and use that description to shape your next sales or marketing strategy.

STAGE 2

KEEP THEM COMING BACK

3

A QUICK GUIDE TO THE CHAPTERS AHEAD

Before we dive into these next few chapters, I'll just quickly share why I set them up this way and the thinking behind my approach. Having covered the business world for 30+ years for publications like *Fortune Small Business, Black Enterprise, Business Insider* and *Hispanic Business,* I know that different companies tackle customer retention from different angles. And, that not all strategies work for every single organization.

Sure there are some similarities across them, but simply using a broad brush to say that "Strategy X" works for all companies overlooks how different businesses operate in the real world. It also does you a disservice as the reader who needs practicable, tangible advice on how to keep your own customers for life.

So with this in mind, I broke the small business arena up into four different categories:

→ **Service businesses** that sell expertise or specialized support and rely on ongoing client relationships rather than one-off projects. This includes consulting firms, accounting practices, IT service providers and other professional services.

→ **Online sellers** that sell products and services through websites, platforms or marketplaces and win repeat business by giving customers product information, simple checkout processes and dependable fulfillment. This sector includes ecommerce brands, digital product businesses, subscription-based models and software-as-a-service (SaaS) providers (among others).

→ **Companies with physical locations** where customers show up in person and experience plays a direct role in whether they return. Retail shops, salons, fitness studios and food trucks all fall into this group, even when mobility is part of the model.

→ **Freelance and gig businesses** built around individual skill sets, where reputation and responsiveness often matter more than scale. Writers, designers, consultants and independent contractors fit here.

These categories give you a starting point, not a label. You may read through this list and feel like your business doesn't belong in any one bucket at all, and that's okay. In fact, many businesses don't fit cleanly into a single category. For example:

- A service firm may also sell digital products.
- An online brand may have a physical storefront.
- A freelancer may provide a subscription or software offering.

Start with the chapters that line up best with how your business operates and use the rest as reference points.

What Comes Next and Why

To keep the next four chapters easy to follow and genuinely useful, I organized each one in the same manner. That way, once you get your bearings in the first chapter, you'll know exactly what to expect from the rest. Each chapter is broken into four sections:

1) **Where retention slips.** We start by looking at common issues that interfere with customer retention. These are the

problems that chip away at loyalty over time, often without anyone noticing until customers stop coming back.

2) **The opportunities standing in front of you.** Next, we look at what's already working in your favor. Every business model comes with built-in opportunities to strengthen customer relationships, even if those tactics aren't completely obvious. I'll help you uncover some that you may have overlooked.

3) **The strategies that actually move the needle.** This is the core of each chapter. Here, we focus on the retention strategies that hold up in real businesses and make the biggest difference over time, based on how customers in this category behave and what keeps them coming back.

4) **What to do next.** I'll give you specific actions to take in your own business so you can start improving retention and building customer relationships that stick.

Each chapter also includes interactive elements like short quizzes, checklists and simple self-assessments. I've also included real-life stories from my own experience and from people I've interviewed over the years to show what these ideas look like in the business world.

With that roadmap in mind, we'll kick off with service businesses. Ready? Let's go.

4

ELEVATE YOUR SERVICE BUSINESS

The service business category covers a wide range of companies that sell expertise, knowledge, intellectual property and other assets that can't be seen, touched or sized up like a product. The service sector in the U.S. is huge and currently makes up about 80% of all organizations. In fact, the vast majority of the 33 million+ small enterprises currently operating in the U.S. are service businesses.

According to the U.S. Census Bureau and the Bureau of Labor Statistics, most small service businesses cluster in a handful of broad categories. The largest groups include professional and business services like consulting, accounting and marketing; health care and social assistance; administrative and support services; food and personal care services; real estate and rental services; transportation and delivery; information and technology services; and education and training.

These companies deal with some unique customer retention challenges. A lot of their work is relationship-driven, customized and difficult to standardize or systematize. At boutique firms, for example, most of the processes and approaches may live in their founders' heads. This makes it difficult to scale up, find new customers and keep existing ones. If you add issues like inconsistent communication, pricing sensitivity and long gaps between engagements to the equation, even satisfied customers can slip away unnoticed.

On a positive note, service companies are really well positioned to keep customers for life because trust compounds over time. Once a client finds a provider that understands their needs, delivers consistently and makes the relationship easy to maintain, switching may feel risky and inconvenient. Service businesses also have more natural touchpoints to reinforce value, solve problems early and deepen relationships in ways product-based companies often can't. When done well, service creates familiarity, confidence and continuity—all building blocks of long-term customer loyalty.

For proof, we can look to the fee-only financial planning field, which I worked with for 20+ years as a journalist for *NAPFA Advisor* (the magazine for the National Association of Personal Financial Advisors, a trade organization focused on expanding the use of fee-only financial advisors by individual consumers). I wrote monthly member profiles for *NAPFA Advisor* for firms of all sizes, although most of them were smaller outfits run by their founders and maybe a handful of advisors, employees and assistants. Some started in their founders' homes and later moved out into office space while others were still being run from home.

These folks ran the gamut, but at their core they were all service businesses building customers for life. Their approach was rock solid and often spanned generations of the same family, professionals from similar occupations or individuals looking for like-minded advisors to handle their finances. Once they hit their strides, most NAPFA members not only held onto their clients literally for life, but generally always had some kind of "waiting list" and velvet rope approach to accepting new ones.

So what's their secret sauce? A lot of it is weaved right into their business models. After all, picking up and moving financial planners is no easy task. Once you find a good one you're likely to stick with that person or firm. All of the NAPFA members I interviewed also pride themselves on having bucked the commission-based investment model and instead charge clear, transparent fees for their work. That structure gives them the freedom to focus on advice over transactions and work closely with each client, regardless of portfolio size or product potential.

But structure alone doesn't explain the loyalty. What really stands out is how deliberately these firms manage relationships. They set expectations early, communicate consistently and make clients feel known, seen and appreciated. Many of these firms were also among the first to use tools like videoconferencing, which allowed them to reach more clients without losing the personal feel of the relationship. Videoconferencing also made meetings easier to schedule, reduced extra steps for busy clients and extended the life of the advisor-client relationship even as people moved to different states, changed jobs or entered new stages of life.

NAPFA members don't keep customers for life by accident. They do it by designing their businesses around long-term relationships. The good news is you don't have to be a financial planner to apply that thinking. The same principles show up repeatedly in service businesses that manage to keep customers by:

- Delivering a solid experience
- Communicating clearly
- Making the relationship easy to maintain over time

People also expect the experience to feel familiar from one interaction to the next, even when different staff handle the work. Think about the HVAC tech, electrician or plumber that you call on when you need something. The familiarity counts way more than saving a few bucks by shopping around, right? Customers of service companies share the same sentiment and they also:

→ Look for predictable communication, especially around timing, pricing and next steps. When my HVAC company tried using an AI chatbot to direct customer service calls last year, I instantly started thinking about alternate providers (they've thankfully gone back to human operators after that failed experiment).

→ Notice small variations and start to raise questions about reliability when those changes stack up over time. Your best customers aren't going to drop you when you try to improve or enhance your service offering, but no one really likes it when you move their cheese. Be sure to ladder in small variations over time, not all at once.

→ Want to buy from businesses that deliver steady experiences and, as a result, earn more trust than those that only overdeliver occasionally (who doesn't want more "white glove" service in their lives?).

→ Don't expect a strong follow-up process, but they notice when one exists. Most service businesses don't put much effort into follow-up, so doing it well gives you an edge.

Service businesses stand out when they do what their name implies: deliver steady service, reliable follow-through and communication clients can depend on. They reduce hassle by walking clients through the process before work begins, explaining what happens next, when clients will hear from them again and where things could change. They flag delays early and talk through cost changes as they happen. When these expectations stay aligned, relationships last longer.

Let's Map the Customer Relationship

Before moving on, take one long-term customer and walk through the relationship from that customer's point of view.

1) How did this customer first find you?
2) What made this customer choose you over other options?
3) How did the first 30 days of the relationship go?
4) At any point did the work start to feel familiar rather than transactional?
5) What would this customer lose if the relationship ended tomorrow?
6) What part of the relationship would be hardest to replace?

Use this exercise to figure out where your customer relationships are strong and where they need work. If you can answer these questions clearly, you've probably got a retention path already, even if it's not formal. If some answers feel vague or you're guessing, those gaps are usually where companies lose customers. That's where attention drops off, follow-up stops happening and relationships end.

The Case for Extreme Customer Service

When responses lag, follow-ups fall through or issues bounce around unresolved, clients notice and remember those moments. They may not complain this time, but they will file those poor experiences away in their minds. The next small slip registers not as a one-off, but as a pattern they've already started to suspect. As someone whose run a service business for 30+ years I can tell you this: when this happens, you won't always have a chance to course-correct. Clients rarely announce their frustration or offer a warning shot before they move on, especially in markets where competition is stiff and the list of available providers is long.

One way to shield yourself from this issue is by becoming part of your customers' operation or, in the case of the NAPFA planners, their lives. When your work plugs directly into how a client runs a business or manages daily life, you stop being a "nice-to-have" and start being part of the machinery. Replacing you would mean rebuilding context, re-explaining history and recreating rhythm, none of which anyone has time for in today's busy world. Most people stick with what already works because it's the easier path. For service business owners, that inertia works in your favor and becomes another pillar in building customers for life.

10 Warning Signs of a Service Relationship Breakdown

We've all seen it happen. Even the most seasoned service firms can lose their footing when standards slip, communication weakens or value becomes assumed instead of reinforced. Use this checklist to pressure-test how your client relationships are holding up.

- ☑ **Inconsistent service quality.** Different people deliver different experiences with no clear standard.

- ☑ **Slow response times without explanation.** Delays become normal and no one resets expectations.

☑ **No one takes ownership when clients have questions.** Requests bounce around or stall without resolution.

☑ **Unresolved issues come up again and again.** No one ever closes the loop.

☑ **Communication happens only when there's a deadline or problem.** Proactive updates disappear once work gets underway.

☑ **Clients don't understand what they're paying for.** You assume the value you're delivering is obvious, but it's not.

☑ **Service feels generic vs. tailored.** The work stops reflecting and catering to the individual clients and their needs, wants and preferences.

☑ **Expectations vary depending on who's talking.** Processes live in people's heads instead of in systems that team members can access and use.

☑ **Client engagement fades without open feedback.** Meetings shorten, responses thin out and participation drops.

☑ **Customers leave without saying why.** The business tracks churn, but doesn't really know why it's happening.

These warning signs rarely appear in isolation. When several pop up together, the relationship is starting to slip. But if you catch them early, you've got room to make changes. You can strengthen communication, spell out the value more clearly or improve your follow-up while the client is still invested in working with you.

Steps to Take Right Now

If you want your clients to stick around longer, start with what you can control this week. Write down what a new client experiences in the first month, including onboarding, scheduling, communication, billing and follow-up. Look for gaps where a client might be left wondering what's happening or what comes next. The goal is to make the first 30 days of the relationship feel organized and intentional.

Next, commit to one consistent follow-up. Use a short email, call or check-in to confirm the work turned out as expected and to address any open questions or concerns. This one move can flag problems you wouldn't see coming until it's too late.

Lastly, study a handful of clients who have stayed with you the longest. Pay attention to how you onboarded them, communicated with them and structured the work. Then, compare that experience to shorter relationships. The difference usually explains where retention breaks down and shows you what needs fixing.

Keeping clients long-term isn't complicated. It's about doing a few things well and not letting them slide. Service businesses lose clients when relationships run on autopilot, but keep them when the work delivers on its promises, communication lines stay open and someone on your team stays accountable. Nail those and your clients won't start wondering if the grass is greener somewhere else.

Put This Chapter to Work By:

☞ **Mapping the first 30 days of a new client relationship.** Include onboarding, scheduling, communication, billing and follow-up.

☞ **Standardizing how service is delivered and explained.** Define what "good service" looks like so the experience feels familiar no matter who handles the work.

☞ **Watching for early warning signs of churn.** Use the checklist in this chapter to spot inconsistent service, slow responses and fading engagement.

☞ **Creating a simple service punch list and using it for every client.** Document the key steps from first contact through follow-up so nothing gets skipped or handled differently.

 **Make This Your Next Step**
Choose one service standard and make it non-negotiable across your entire customer base.

5

DRIVE MORE ONLINE SALES

E-commerce went from fringe to fundamental almost overnight. Online sales in the U.S. now account for over 16% of total retail sales, meaning roughly one in every six retail dollars happens through a screen rather than in a store. As of 2026, online channels made up about 20% of total worldwide retail sales as digital buying became standard behavior rather than a novelty.

This change blew the doors open for pretty much anyone who had a good idea and a viable product or service behind it. No more leases, office space or foot traffic needed. The combination of social platforms and accessible e-commerce tools created new paths for:

➤ **Makers of handmade gifts and home décor** who used to rely mostly on craft fairs, seasonal markets and local word of mouth to sell their wares. Online storefronts gave them a window to the world, allowing them to sell year-round, reach a global audience and increase income streams beyond in-person events.

➤ **Artists and designers** who sell prints, jewelry and original work without galleries, pop-ups or retail partners. Digital shops give them control over pricing, presentation and customer relationships and lessen dependency on middlemen who used to control both the sale and the end customer relationship.

➤ **Small product brands** that launch direct-to-consumer instead of starting with wholesale. Entrepreneurs can readily test products, refine packaging and adjust pricing in real time based on customer behavior.

> ➤ **Software companies** selling self-serve (SaaS) tools and subscriptions directly through their own websites and app marketplaces. Customers sign up, pay and get started on their own, with the entire transaction happening online rather than through a traditional software sales process.

> ➤ **First-time entrepreneurs** looking for a simpler path into the retail selling space. Platforms handle payments, logistics and basic infrastructure so startups can focus on product development and visibility.

> ➤ **Service professionals** who turn expertise into products, including coaches, consultants and educators selling digital downloads, templates, courses or tools. E-commerce gives them a way to package knowledge, reach wider audiences and generate repeat sales.

This list isn't exhaustive, but you get the gist: e-commerce put the power of entrepreneurship in a lot of people's hands. And it continues to with one big caveat: the internet is now a pretty crowded place. Customers can compare options, prices and reviews in seconds, and switching sellers takes almost no effort, a dynamic explored in more depth in this book's Introduction.

The e-commerce boom also made customer retention a bit trickier. "Running an e-commerce business is a bit like hosting a party. You want plenty of new faces coming through the door, but if no one sticks around, you're just left with an empty dance floor and a lot of wasted punch," Funnel's Sean Dougherty writes. "The secret to a lively, thriving event? Getting your guests to stay for another song, or in the case of e-commerce, convincing your customers to come back for another purchase."

Getting buyers to "stick around for another song" isn't always easy for e-commerce companies that are operating in a sea of similar products and lookalike listings. In this environment, customers leave because you didn't give them any reason to return. Sure the order arrived and the transaction closed, but the relationship ended there.

You <u>Can</u> Keep the Party Alive After the First Sale

If you look at order delivery as the midpoint of the race vs. finish line, you'll already be ahead of sellers who treat the transaction as the end of the relationship. A few Christmases ago, my daughter gifted me an acoustic guitar ordered online from Sweetwater. The box included a handwritten note, a free bag of candy (nice touch) and clear follow-up information. They added me to their email list, and a few days later someone from Sweetwater called to confirm if it arrived safely and to ask whether I needed help tuning it or getting started. I've since bought accessories and other gear from them without ever setting foot in their Fort Wayne, Indiana store.

Here's another one that stands out: Every order from Swan Creek Candles includes a handwritten thank-you and a free sample tucked into the box. They stay in touch when new wax melt scents or seasonal products hit the market, which makes reordering feel natural and not forced. These small, personalized touches turned me into a repeat customer. Another company may sell cheaper wax melts, but these guys hooked me for life.

Here's the reality: most e-commerce businesses chase the first sale and then hope customers come back on their own. Unfortunately, this rarely happens on its own. Count how many of these happen after someone buys from you:

- **Customers know what happens after the order ships.** They know the tracking, timing and next steps and are never left guessing.

- **The package itself makes an impression.** Packing, inserts or presentation reinforce your brand and its products instead of feeling purely transactional.

- **There's a human signal post-delivery.** A follow-up email, note or check-in confirms the order arrived and the customer relationship is valuable.

- **Customers hear from you again for a reason.** Post-purchase communication adds value and doesn't come across as salesy.

- **Support feels easy to reach if something goes wrong.** Customers don't have to hunt for help or send multiple messages.

- **The next purchase feels obvious.** Accessories, refills or related products naturally follow the original order.

- **Repeat customers feel recognized.** The experience doesn't reset every time they come back with another order.

- **Email or messaging stays relevant.** Updates match what customers actually bought, care about and need.

- **Your brand stays present without being pushy.** Communication keeps you top of mind without forcing urgency or pestering your best customers.

- **The relationship doesn't end at delivery.** Customers have a reason to stay connected long after that first box arrives.

If you're already doing most of these things, great. That means you're not leaving the relationship to chance after delivery. You've built habits that give customers reasons to come back without being pushed or chased. If only a handful apply, the foundation is there, but the experience stops too early. Tightening up a few post-purchase touchpoints will help spur more repeat orders and lifelong customers.

If you need more help in this area, start by deciding what should happen after every order and <u>making it consistent</u>. When customers know what to expect and hear from you again for a reason, staying connected becomes an easy choice. But when you drop off the map and fade into the great internet abyss, customers won't think of you the next time they need a holiday gift for a musician or wax melts for their candle warmer.

Winning Online Customers for Life

Most online businesses obsess over traffic, ads and conversion rates. They want to know how many eyeballs are on their storefronts, how many browsers turned into buyers and how long those buyers spent on each page. Far fewer businesses pay the same attention to what happens after the order confirmation hits the inbox. This approach makes sense on some levels, but it's a costly blind spot in a market where customers expect attention, personalization and follow-through.

For help in this area, we can look to some of the largest brands that had enough money, resources and IT firepower to master the e-commerce game early. Walmart, Target and of course Amazon stand as three obvious examples. Their success in the online selling arena didn't happen overnight; it happened when all three invested in the convenience, scale and repeatable buying experiences that we've since become accustomed to.

Most small businesses don't have the budgets, teams or desire to take on Amazon or Walmart, but they can still borrow a page from their playbooks. Strip away the scale and what's left are the practical strategies that all businesses can use to stand out, acquire customers and keep them for life.

Here are 15 ways online businesses can apply those same ideas without needing Amazon-sized budgets or teams:

1) **Make repeat buying the easiest option.** If customers have to start from scratch every time, many won't bother coming back, so reduce effort by adding one-click reorders, saved carts or "buy again" buttons in emails. Even a simple reorder link in a shipping confirmation can make a difference.

2) **Tell customers exactly what happens after checkout.** Uncertainty erodes confidence, which directly affects customer retention. Use confirmation emails to share shipping timelines, explain what updates customers will receive and clearly point them to support if something goes wrong.

3) **Design the experience around the second purchase.** Many e-commerce sites treat conversion as the finish line, leaving the post-purchase experience underdeveloped. Use follow-up emails to suggest related products, share usage tips or send refill reminders that make the next purchase feel natural.

4) **Recognize returning customers.** Loyalty is built through subtle signals, not big announcements, so offer early access, exclusive content or small perks visible only to logged-in users. Let the experience communicate appreciation without calling attention to it.

5) **Remove customer hesitation points.** Every extra step gives customers a reason to leave and not return, so simplify checkout, shorten forms and avoid confusing policies. Your support inbox is a good place to start looking for those problem areas.

6) **Make returns simple and predictable.** When returns feel manageable, customers are more willing to buy again. Publish easily understandable return rules, automate labels and process refunds quickly.

7) **Stay useful after the sale.** Send short how-to emails, care tips or reminders tied to what they purchased. This keeps your brand relevant without pushing a sale.

8) **Use personalization only where it adds value.** Base recommendations on actual behavior like past purchases or timing. Apparel brands track what size someone bought last time to make the next purchase easier. Personal care brands send reminders when customers are likely running low.

9) **Create one small moment of surprise.** Memorable experiences usually come from small, unexpected touches, such as a handwritten note, bonus item or genuine thank-you message.

10) **Fix problems promptly.** Customers are paying attention to how issues are handled. Respond quickly, explain what happened and make the resolution straightforward.

11) **Give customers a reason to return soon.** If too much time passes, customers forget why they bought from you. Timing-based reminders, replenishment prompts or "most customers reorder now" messages keep you on their radar.

12) **Make referrals feel natural, not salesy.** People share brands when it feels helpful, not transactional, so keep rewards simple and mutual. Place referral prompts after positive moments like reviews or repeat orders.

13) **Pay attention to customers who ghost without notice.** Churn usually starts silently, so track customers who haven't returned in 60 or 90 days and reach out with a

useful check-in. Waiting too long makes it harder to get them back into the fold.

14) **Communicate with restraint and purpose.** All of our email inboxes are overflowing, so send messages or texts sparingly. If it doesn't help your customer, don't send it.

15) **Choose consistent over clever.** Retention is built on trust, and trust comes from knowing what to expect. If fulfillment, communication and support work predictably, customers don't have to rethink their decision to buy from you again.

Here's the bottom line: customer retention in the online world isn't about clever tactics or chasing the latest platform feature. It's about paying attention to what happens after someone chooses you and then caring about what happens next. Most of these strategies aren't complicated or expensive, but they do require consistency and follow-through. Build your own strategy one step at a time, starting with making it easier and reassuring for customers to come back to you versus start over somewhere else.

Make Checkout a Transition, Not a Finish Line

Online sellers cover a broad swath that includes everyone from solo makers shipping a handful of orders each week to product brands moving real volume every day, and all steps in between. Not all of these companies use (or even need to use) the same retention tactics, but here are a few good starting points any business can use.

First, map out the first couple of weeks after an order is placed, from confirmation and shipping updates to delivery and follow-up. Look for points where customers are left guessing about timing, tracking or what comes next. Find ways to eliminate or minimize those complications. Often, the fix is just clearer communication and an easy way for customers to reach you.

Next, decide on one post-delivery follow-up routine and make it non-negotiable. That could be a short message confirming the order arrived, a practical tip tied to the product (similar to Sweetwater's approach with my guitar delivery) or a simple check-in that signals the relationship didn't end at checkout.

Lastly, select one small group of customers who've come back on their own. Look at what they bought first, how long it took them to reorder and how your company communicated with them in between. Then compare that experience to customers who haven't come back and flag the specific emails, touchpoints or handoffs that were missing or delayed. Even subtle changes in this area can improve customer retention rates.

In the end, the businesses that win online are paying attention to what happens after the sale. For them, checkout is a transition and not a finish line. Get this part right and repeat purchases become the natural outcome, not something you have to push for.

Put This Chapter to Work By:

☞ **Pinpointing what happens after every order.** Write down the exact sequence from confirmation to delivery to follow-up and fix the points where customers are left guessing or forgotten.

☞ **Automating one post-delivery follow-up and making it non-negotiable.** Choose a single message that adds value after the order arrives and set it up to go out every time, without relying on memory or manual effort.

☞ **Making repeat customers feel recognized without calling attention to it.** Use small signals like saved preferences, early access or tailored recommendations.

☞ **Closing the gaps where communication comes to a halt.** Look at where emails, messages or outreach drop off after the first sale and tighten those handoffs before customers leave for good.

Make This Your Next Step
Pull one recent order, read every message the customer received after checkout and fix the first moment where the experience started to feel forgettable.

6

GET MORE FOOT TRAFFIC INTO YOUR PHYSICAL LOCATION

I'm not even a big makeup wearer, but I'm a raving Sephora fan for one reason that dates back about 20 years. I went into their downtown Seattle store to grab something and when I got to the check out, the employee's eyes lit up and she flashed a big smile as soon as my customer profile popped up on her screen. "It's your birthday month!" she proclaimed with gusto. "And here's your free gift." She reached under the counter, pulled out a set of three lip glosses and handed them to me.

And with that, I became a lifelong Sephora customer. Why? Well because no one had ever done anything like that for me before, and the experience was so impactful that I'm still talking and writing about it 20 years later. I continue to shop there and have spawned an equally enthusiastic customer (and, lover of the annual birthday gift presentation) in my own daughter.

I feel the same about Gucci, which is one of those places where even if you walk into their flagship stop on Rodeo Drive in jeans and a t-shirt (been there, done that), they still treat you like a celebrity who just rolled up in a Bugatti. And somehow every employee across that entire organization (or at least the ones I've interacted with anyway) shares that welcoming attitude. We've had employees at the Las Vegas store show us secret drawers of marked-down bags and ones in Honolulu bring us champagne for buying a single belt.

Wish I could say the same about all luxury brands. I won't name any names, but it's pretty obvious that customer service as whole has fallen off so badly that the companies that still commit to it stick out like sore thumbs. This is your shot to be the exception in your field, whether you're running a clinic, bookstore, pop-up shop or other business customers visit face-to-face.

This chapter focuses on those types of companies but also includes mobile businesses. Food truck owners, mobile dog groomers, mobile fitness trainers and on-site service providers all have to make real investments in vehicles, equipment and operating infrastructure in order to operates. Whether customers come to you or you go to them, the economics are similar.

The details change, but the pressure doesn't: real-world costs don't go away, and repeat customers keep them manageable.

Put Personal Touchpoints to Work

Brick-and-mortar companies have a distinct advantage over their virtual brethren, who rarely see, seldom speak to and only occasionally communicate directly with their customers. This applies universally these days, and it's why my son-in-law's best job offer was from the one company (out of 300-plus applications and countless interviews) that he went to visit in person. Face-to-face still matters, even in a digital world.

Physical businesses have their own challenges to navigate. Customer retention ebbs and flows based on the economy and broader trends. The evolution of the American mall shows how much things can shift. This age-old mainstay looks nothing like it did 20 years ago. And even at a time where people crave more connectivity and touchpoints, the mall is just a shadow of its former self.

These shifts affect all kinds of physical businesses. Here are some of the top customer retention challenges that companies with physical, mobile or stationary locations are facing:

→ **Service varies depending on the day or shift.** A restaurant feels welcoming on Friday night and rushed on Tuesday afternoon. A retail store is helpful one week and checked out the next. Customers notice the inconsistency even if they don't complain about it.

→ **Staff turnover impacts relationships.** Regulars don't just come back for products or menus. They come back for familiar faces. When those disappear, loyalty often goes out the door with them.

→ **Businesses don't actually track who's coming back.** Owners rely on recognition and memory, which works until it doesn't. By the time someone realizes a customer hasn't been in for months, they're already gone.

→ **Heavy reliance on discounts and price cuts.** Restaurants, retailers, food trucks and other businesses use discounts to attract business, then wonder why customers only show up when there's a deal attached.

→ **Customer service drops when things get busy.** Long waits, late starts and slow checkouts always seem to rear their heads when places are most crowded and customers have little or no patience to spare.

→ **The relationship ends the moment the transaction does.** A sale closes, a dog grooming session ends, a service wraps up and communication stops. There's no follow-up, no reminder and no reason to return.

→ **Customers lost to logistics.** There's one food truck in my area that I love, but if I don't know where it's going to be on a Friday night, I probably won't make the effort to track it down myself.

→ **What's online doesn't match the in-person experience.** This is a big one that even large brick and mortar retailers grapple with. Menus, product descriptions, photos and reviews set expectations. When the real thing looks nothing like what was promised, customer trust erodes fast.

When one or more of these scenarios happen, brick-and-mortar customers slip out without making a fuss, complaining, writing a negative review or announcing their exit. They just stop showing up, calling, setting appointments and patronizing your business. Online companies can see this happening in real time through dashboards and data; physical businesses usually can't. The warning signs are subtle, but they're usually right in front of you every day on the floor, at the counter or during a service call. A regular who used to come in twice a week now shows up once a month. Someone who always asked for you by name starts working with whoever's available. A loyal customer stops engaging the way they used to. It's easy to miss these signals if you're not watching for them.

Do the Work for Your Customers

Customers stick around when you get the basics right every time they show up. Research from MIT Sloan consistently shows that customers who feel recognized, respected and confident about what to expect are far more likely to return than those who simply complete a satisfactory transaction. For physical businesses, that insight matters even more because loyalty is built in person, one interaction at a time.

"In-store shopping isn't just about picking up a needed item. It's a social experience and an opportunity to physically gather with friends," MIT's Sharmila C. Chatterjee writes. "People of all ages enjoy touching and trying out new products. While online shopping may be convenient, shopping in-person provides valuable social interaction and immediate gratification when shoppers leave with products in hand."

Smart companies understand this and also know that customers will repeat the process if they had a good experience and their needs met. This is a great opportunity to design for the second (and subsequent) visit. In fact, you should plan always backward from the second visit by asking yourself what makes it easy, natural or obvious for someone to come back. A restaurant might mention a weekly special at the end of the meal, for example, or a salon can pre-book the next appointment before the customer leaves (borrow a page from your dentist on that one).

Similarly, a mobile dog groomer might leave behind a card that states how far out bookings typically fill or a retail store—borrowing a page from Kohl's—can hand a customer a coupon to use on their next visit while they're still standing in front of them. When that next step is obvious, customers don't have to remember you. You've already done that work for them. And trust me, it works. Every time I get a $20 Kohl's Cash good for a future visit I'm already planning my next trip there before I leave the store. That's what you're aiming for: planting that seed for the next visit before this one's even over.

10-Point Customer Retention Quiz

Answer each of these with a simple yes or no, with no being a sign that your customer retention strategy needs an overhaul:

1) Do customers know what happens after their visit?

2) Does your service feel similar regardless of who's working?

3) Do you have an easy way to spot regulars versus first-timers?

4) Is there a natural moment to invite customers back?

5) Would a customer notice if they didn't hear from you again?

6) Do customers know how to reach you easily if something goes wrong after they leave?

7) Does your business feel easy to return to without re-explaining everything each time?

8) Do repeat customers get any subtle signal that you recognize them?

9) Are busy periods managed in a way that doesn't punish loyal customers for showing up?

10) If a regular stopped coming in for 60 or 90 days, would you notice?

How to Close Gaps that Lose Customers

If you answered "no" to some of the questions in the quiz, you're probably leaving retention to chance. This is a fairly common problem for companies that have physical locations and that rely on foot traffic and face-to-face interactions. Owners assume loyalty lives in a customer's head when it actually lives in the experience.

When retention starts slipping, most businesses react the same way. They post more on social. They run discounts. They add another tech tool. The problem is that none of that works if the experience itself feels forgettable. A food truck loses customers when people don't know where it'll be. A shop loses them when service depends on who's working. A gym loses customers when nothing happens after signup.

If these challenges sound familiar, it's time to stop assuming customers will come back and start making it easier for them to do so. The good news is that unlike virtual companies, you have direct connections. You know your customers and they know you. In many cases, they already like you and want to come back. It's just a matter of giving them a clear path and a reason to take it.

Create an Uncluttered Path Back to Your Door

First, decide what the "next visit" looks like for your business. This sounds basic, but many physical businesses never define it.

➤ Is the next step another meal within a week?

➤ A rebooking within six weeks?

➤ A new menu item or service offering you're rolling out soon?

➤ A standing appointment?

Pick one and make sure every customer hears about it before they leave your place. Restaurants can mention a weekly special or upcoming event as the check hits the table. Salons and groomers can pre-book the next appointment while the customer is still in the chair. Retailers can point out what usually pairs with today's purchase or what's arriving soon.

Next, standardize and automate one simple follow-up. It doesn't have to be overly clever or long, but it does have to happen every time. It can be:

- A short thank-you text after a service call.

- A quick email the day after a visit that confirms hours, contact info or how to book again.

- A printed card at checkout that explains how far in advance bookings usually fill.

- A sticker reminding a car owner when their next oil change is due.

- A text sharing a mobile business' weekly route.

The goal here is continuity. When customers feel remembered, they'll remember you in return.

Lastly, pay attention to who comes back and who doesn't, then change one thing. You don't need a complicated system either. Just a simple list will do. Ask yourself: Who returned within 30 or 60 days? Who hasn't? Look for patterns instead of perfection. Did regulars book before leaving? Did first-time customers get any follow-up at all? Did busy days feel rushed while slower days felt personal?

Now pick one gap and fix it. That might mean investing in a point of sale (POS) system that gets people through checkout faster, doing a better job of noticing regulars or being clear about what comes next, once the sale wraps up. In a physical business, these small operational changes matter more than big, expensive ideas. Build them into your daily operations and customer loyalty will follow.

Put This Chapter to Work By:

☞ **Putting real face time to good use.** Don't let the visit end without setting up what comes next, whether that's a return date, a reason to check back or a simple reminder.

☞ **Turning the end of an interaction into a handoff, not a goodbye.** What you say or do in the final two minutes matters more than anything you post online or send out afterward.

☞ **Letting your POS system do some of the remembering for you.** When regulars don't have to reintroduce themselves every time, the experience feels easier and more personal without extra effort from staff.

☞ **Fixing the one moment customers see when you're under pressure.** Busy lines, rushed service or awkward wrap-ups can erode customer loyalty over time.

Make This Your Next Step

Pay attention to how customers leave and ask yourself this question: What can we do to make coming back feel like a natural next step?

7

KEEP YOUR GIG & FREELANCE PIPELINE FULL

Last but definitely not least is a business sector that's near and dear to my heart, and one that was so new when I started out that the phrase "gig economy" had yet to be coined and most people assumed that if you were working from home it meant you were a housewife (true story). There were support groups for the tiny group of work-from-homers and author Paul and Sarah Edwards owned the space with their *Working From Home* handbook, which was first published in the mid-1980s. We all read the book, learned from it and followed their lead on how to set up and run a business from home.

The landscape looks nothing like it did back then, but I still have the very first freelance magazine client that I started working with in the early-1990s. The lesson here is that even though we've changed tools, platforms and how we find work, the way long-term freelance relationships are built hasn't really changed at all.

As freelancers and gig-economy workers operating outside traditional employment, we don't keep clients by chasing every new platform or constantly pitching to strangers. We keep them by being reliable and easy to work with. Do that consistently and clients stop thinking of you as a vendor and start treating you like part of their operation.

Here's How it Usually Goes Down

Freelancers and gig economy workers face some unique challenges on the customer retention front. As someone who has worked in this space for 30+ years, I've seen:

- **Large clients disappear overnight, even after years of steady work.** I've worked with global software companies that called on me to create programs and content for years, then went silent with zero warning. Not because the work wasn't good or the relationship soured, but because a budget shifted, a strategy changed or a new leader decided to take things in a different direction. There was no warning or heads up. One day the work was there, the next day an entirely new team had taken over and didn't need outside writing support anymore. That's not a knock on those companies; it's just the reality of being outside the decision-making circle.

- **Some clients invest heavily upfront and then vanish after one assignment.** I've had situations where a company spent an enormous amount of time onboarding me, looping me into systems, explaining processes and getting me "ready to roll," only to assign one project and then fade out. I followed up, checked in and stayed available, but nothing came of it. The preparation far outweighed the payoff, and there was no clear reason why. That kind of imbalance is frustrating, but it's also common in independent work.

- **Effort and return don't always align.** More time, more planning and more effort don't automatically lead to more revenue when you're working independently. I've seen small, well-defined projects turn into some of the most profitable work I've done, while large, sprawling engagements dragged on for months and barely moved the needle financially. That unevenness isn't a failure on your part. It's part of how freelance and gig work functions.

These scenarios are all pretty much par for the course, but that doesn't make the customer retention bit any easier for us. When you work independently, you're close enough to do the work but far enough away from the decisions that control budgets, priorities and timelines. Freelancers, contractors and gig workers don't usually get advance notice when those decisions shift, but we do feel the impact after it hits.

So what does this mean for customer retention? For one, client relationships in independent work fade when the workflow shuts off, priorities shift or budgets tighten up. Nothing has to be technically "wrong," but there's also nothing moving the relationship forward. Over time, this complacency translates into customer churn.

Now I'm not saying we have it any harder than anyone else does, but being outside of the "circle of trust" while being treated as a trusted part of the team you're supporting is an interesting position to be in. Freelancers, contractors and gig workers live in that in-between space, where responsibility is high but visibility into decisions is limited.

The good news is that for the most part, independent contractors fill a void left by internal constraints. Companies hire freelancers, contractors and gig workers when they don't have the time, bandwidth or specific expertise in-house. That need doesn't disappear just because a project pauses or priorities shift. This alone creates a baseline level of customer retention. If you play your hand right, it may become a relationship that lasts for years and not just a single assignment.

Creating "Easy Yes" Moments

Here's a great way to either reframe or lay out a new customer retention strategy. Think about a recent client or project. Now imagine this: six months from now, that client has a new need. What makes it easy for them to say yes to working with you again?

→ A clear understanding of what you do best

→ Familiarity with how you work

→ Confidence you'll deliver without surprises

→ No need to re-explain their business

→ Clear boundaries around scope and expectations

→ A track record they don't have to second-guess

→ An easy way to restart the conversation

→ A sense that you'll make their job easier

→ Trust that you'll flag issues before they become problems

→ A natural next step they can picture, even if they're not ready yet

Every item on this list comes down to one thing: when clients decide to offload more work to an independent contractor, they're not debating skill or personality. They're deciding how much work it will take to restart the relationship. Having to re-explain context, micromanage details or worry about unknowns can all drive your clients to consider other options.

Get the Work Off Your Client's Desk

Most companies don't hire independent contractors because they're looking for a relationship. They hire us because they need something done, often quickly, without adding headcount or internal complexity. That's the opening for you. Retention happens when you handle that need in a way that makes coming back feel natural rather than disruptive.

Based on my own experience, clients come back to self-starters who don't require extra explanation, management or follow-up. This makes sense based on the real reason they outsource in the first place: to get the work off their desk and onto yours (either figuratively or literally, depending on your specific industry and business model).

There are many ways that an independent contractor can prove their worth and foster long-term client loyalty. Most of these have nothing to do with selling yourself and everything to do with how you operate once the work is underway. Here's a 20-point punch list of the habits and behaviors that I've found support better, longer-lasting client relationships:

1. Agree on what "done" looks like upfront.

2. Put scope, deadlines and deliverables in writing.

3. Communicate the way the client prefers.

4. Share progress without being asked.

5. Raise problems early instead of waiting.

6. Ask for feedback while work is in progress.

7. Accept feedback without taking it personally.

8. Deliver work when you say you will.

9. Leave room for review by getting done ahead of schedule.

10. Reset expectations when requests change.

11. Recommend simpler or faster approaches.

12. Fix issues without creating new ones.

13. Make it easy for clients to pay.

14. Send clear, predictable invoices.

15. Keep track of client preferences.

16. End projects with a definitive finish.

17. Check in without asking for work.

18. Let clients know you're available.

19. Handle criticism calmly and professionally.

20. Follow through on all of your commitments.

Do these things consistently and clients stop shopping, second-guessing and looking elsewhere. You become the go-to resource they rely on when the work matters and the clock is ticking, and you get clients for life.

Be Your Clients' Pressure Relief Valve

A startup company hires a freelance marketer because it needs momentum without a full-time salary. A hospital brings in a contract IT specialist because it needs expertise fast without retraining staff. A publisher hires a freelance editor because it needs reliable output without managing another employee. In every case, the common thread is the same: they're buying relief, not just skill. You're the pressure relief valve because you offer support, reliability and follow-through at a time when your client either lacks the in-house capacity, is in a rush or just doesn't want to deal with it.

Knowing where you stand is also important. Sure, I didn't know that the large software firm I was engaged with for 4+ years was going to pull the plug on one of its core marketing programs, but I always knew my place in the scheme of things. It's about knowing where your role ends and where the client's internal constraints begin. You can deliver strong work, show up consistently and make yourself valuable, but you can't control budgets, leadership changes or shifting priorities. Recognizing this helps keep expectations realistic, protects the relationship and prevents overreliance on any one client.

The good news is that companies come back to outside contractors who can ease pressure without creating new dependencies or demands. When working with you feels like the least complicated option, keeping the relationship going is an easy decision. That's how repeat work happens, even as priorities, budgets and teams continue to shift.

Position Yourself for Repeat Work

List every client you've worked with in the last year or two, including paused or one-off projects. Ask one question for each: How easy would it be for this client to work with me again tomorrow? If the answer involves re-explaining your process, tracking down old details or renegotiating basics, that's a gap worth fixing.

Next, create a clear path back in. This might be a short check-in, an update on availability or a specific idea tied to their business. A marketer can suggest revisiting a stalled campaign. A designer might flag an asset update. A writer might propose a follow-up piece.

Finally, pay attention to your concentration risk. If most of your income comes from one client, your pipeline is narrow, not full. I've hit this wall many times and have learned how to spot it and avoid it, but not after some tough lessons. Use stable periods to line up additional relationships that could grow over time, even if those engagements start small. This is very important for solo practitioners who can easily get sidelined by an especially high maintenance client, and even as they try to spread their capacity across multiple accounts.

Customers for life come from consistent, dependable execution. Freelancers, independent contractors and gig workers have to make it easy for clients to come back and simple to pick things up again, even if they ghosted for a while. When people know what you deliver, how you operate and what to expect, they return without hesitation. That alone can turn individual projects into clients for life.

Put This Chapter to Work By:

☞ **Taking inventory of recent clients.** List everyone you've worked with in the last 12–24 months and think about what it would take to start working with them again.

☞ **Removing one barrier to reengagement.** Fix a process, handoff or habit that makes coming back to you harder than it needs to be.

☞ **Strengthening your mid-project strategy.** Choose one habit from the punch list that you're not already doing and put it into action.

☞ **Ending projects in a way that encourages continuation.** When you close out the work, make sure clients can easily picture working with you again (even if the timing isn't immediate).

Make This Your Next Step
Create a short, reusable "working with me" document and starting using it with every new and existing client.

STAGE 3

CUSTOMERS FOR LIFE

8

MAKE RETENTION A HABIT, NOT A PHASE

If you take just one thing away from this book, it's that getting and keeping customers for life is not something you can just set and forget. You can't just fix it once, admire your work and move onto the next task. It has to be practiced, adjusted and reinforced over time. And when you own a small or midsized business, you can't afford to take your foot off the gas. Every customer you earn represents real effort, real cost and real risk.

As you learned in earlier chapters, getting a new customer costs money, time, energy and focus. It pulls you into marketing, outreach, selling, onboarding and follow-up, all before you ever get to do the work you actually enjoy or deliver the value you promised. And the minute that customer leaves, you're right back at the starting line, doing it all over again. My goal with this book is to help you move that starting line farther out and spend less time rebuilding what you already earned.

Systems that Hold Up Under Real-World Pressure

I can't just point out why customer retention is hard, hand you a few assessments and call it done. You need ways to make these behaviors stick when things get busy, staff turns over or priorities shift. Every company will handle this differently, but there are some common threads that work across the board.

A CRM is a good starting point for anyone who doesn't have one and wants to do a better job with customer retention. These systems serve as a single source of truth for all customer interactions, buying histories, preferences, customer service issues and more. Trying to remember all of this, using paper-based systems or even capturing it on spreadsheets won't scale as your company grows. These days, most CRMs are available in the cloud on a subscription basis and many of them offer free trial periods for companies that want to test drive the system first.

Your CRM will help you:

⇨ Maintain full client histories in one place instead of hunting through emails, notes or memory.

⇨ Make the information accessible to everyone who needs it, rather than trapped in one person's head or on a spreadsheet on someone's laptop.

⇨ Pick relationships back up smoothly after a pause, handoff or long gap.

⇨ Notice patterns in buying, timing and engagement that are easy to miss otherwise.

⇨ Remember preferences and past issues without relying on sticky notes or gut feel.

⇨ See when a relationship is cooling off before it disappears.

⇨ Follow up with context, not generic check-ins.

⇨ Stay consistent as you grow, even when more people touch the account.

⇨ Avoid losing customer knowledge when roles change or someone leaves.

⇨ Make it easy for returning customers to come back, which makes repeat work more likely.

Along with your CRM, you may want to add:

• A shared calendar or task system to track follow-ups, renewals or check-ins so nothing has to be memorized.

This will help whether you're solopreneur or working with a team.

- A simple documentation space for processes, client preferences or handoff notes. This can be as basic as a shared doc or folder, as long as it's consistent and accessible.

- Basic reporting or dashboards that show repeat purchases, dormant accounts or service issues over time. You don't need complex analytics to spot trends that affect retention.

- Communication tools with history so conversations don't vanish once an email thread gets buried or a team member moves on.

- A regular process for evaluating what's working and what isn't so tools evolve with your business.

8 Ways to Make Customers Stick

Throughout this book, I've mentioned pieces of these systems in different contexts: onboarding, follow-up, communication, service delivery, digital touchpoints and so forth. But I haven't put them all in one spot yet. Here are eight practical processes that work for most businesses, no matter what you sell or how you operate.

A documented "what happens next" process. Every customer relationship should have a defined next step, even when there's no immediate sale or project attached to it. This can be a scheduled review, a reorder window, a renewal conversation or a simple check-in.

A consistent, non-negotiable follow-up cadence. Decide how often customers hear from you and stick with that cadence. Monthly, quarterly or milestone-based all works, but what doesn't work is following up only during a slowdown in sales.

A simple way to capture customer context in real time. Notes, preferences, challenge points and history should get recorded as part of the workflow, not "when there's time." Always record it or capture it in your CRM while the information is fresh.

A standard close-out process for every engagement. Projects, orders and service periods should end cleanly. Summarize what was delivered, what worked and what might come next. Don't let any loose ends or outstanding to-dos linger around unaddressed.

A recurring review of dormant, past customers. Make this a part of your routine client maintenance. Look at who hasn't reordered, renewed or engaged in a while and decide whether action is warranted. Then, take that action.

Clear ownership of the relationship. Even in smaller companies, someone needs to be accountable for each customer relationship. If nobody's paying attention, customers leave.

A feedback process that drives real changes. Collect input from customers through sales calls, service interactions or follow-ups after they buy. Then actually do something with it and let them know.

A regular retention check as part of your overall operations. Retention shouldn't only come up when sales numbers start to slip. Build it into your quarterly planning, team meetings or operational reviews. That way, retention stays visible even when sales are brisk and things are going well.

If you're looking for a good starting point, pick one process from this list, tighten it up and make it non-negotiable. When retention becomes part of how your business runs, customers stop slipping away and start sticking around.

This book helps you hold on to customers in a world where preferences shift constantly, competition never lets up and digital tools keep moving the gameboard pieces. Take what fits your business, skip what doesn't and build the kind of operation people don't want to leave. That's how you turn customers into lifelong relationships instead of one-time transactions.

If you'd like help applying these ideas more directly to your new or growing business, my other two books are a good place to go next. *Your First Business Blueprint* focuses on getting your company started with a structure in place, while *Blueprints Beat Cocktail Napkins* offers an easy, usable approach to business planning. They're both on Amazon and each one builds on the habits and systems you've worked through here. Good luck!

Bridget McCrea

Put This Chapter to Work By:

☞ **Getting one process out of your head and onto paper or screen.** If it only exists in your memory, it won't hold up when things get busy.

☞ **Following through even when there's nothing to sell.** If customers only hear from you when you need something, they'll assume the relationship ends when the transaction closes.

☞ **Building in a regular check for dormant customers.** Skip this step and you'll only notice customer churn after it's already happened.

☞ **Capturing customer context while it's fresh.** If you don't capture it in the moment, it may get watered down or lost altogether.

Make This Your Next Step

Decide which customer relationship you're not willing to rebuild from scratch. Then put one process in place to protect it.

BUSINESS BUILDING RESOURCE HUB

Growing a small business means a lot of learning and finding the right tools to make the process easier. To make things simpler, I've put together a list of resources for you. This list of resources was compiled based on my own research and several other curated resource lists published by the U.S. Chamber of Commerce, S.C.O.R.E and startup savant.

This list is for your information only. I'm not affiliated with any of these sites, companies or tools. They're simply options you can explore as you move through the early stages of business ownership.

Want the clickable version instead? The full list with live links is online at: bridgetmccrea.com/startup-resources

SUPPORT FOR SMALL BUSINESS OWNERS

National Association for the Self-Employed (NASE)
NASE.org
NASE represents companies with 10 employees or fewer. It offers free resources for small business owners and more tools for members, including unlimited access to consultants for tax, retirement, finance and operations questions. NASE also provides a member-only NASE Succeed Scholarship, helping entrepreneurs pay for training programs, business courses and college.

U.S. Small Business Administration (SBA)

SBA.gov

The SBA offers informative content, interactive online tools and a video library for entrepreneurs. These range from business planning solutions to mentoring services and include:

- Small Business Development Centers: Attend in-person events and get individualized assistance from small business centers near you.
- SBA's Ascent: A free online learning platform designed specifically to help women entrepreneurs start, grow and expand their businesses.
- Learning center courses: The SBA's learning center video courses cover starting up to selling your business and everything in between.
- Boots to Business: If you're a transitioning service member (including National Guard and Reserve) or a spouse with access to a military installation, check out the Boots to Business program.

Service Corps of Retired Executives (SCORE)

SCORE.org

SCORE provides resources for small business owners, including webinars, interactive courses, business templates and local workshops. For example, SCORE's Startup Roadmap guides individuals who are starting a new business. An entrepreneur can complete the 12-module step-by-step tutorial alone or with a mentor.

U.S. Chamber of Commerce

Uschamber.com

As the world's largest business organization, the U.S. Chamber of Commerce advocates for

business-friendly policies and provides free resources for entrepreneurs. You'll find many virtual events and informative guides on small business topics and can network within your community by joining a local branch (you can use this directory to find your local Chamber of Commerce).

Minority Business Development Agency (MBDA)

MBDA.gov

The agency supports businesses in minority communities by providing grant and loan information, business opportunities and business certification resources. It links minority-owned businesses with the capital, contracts and markets they need to grow. The MBDA also advocates and promotes minority-owned businesses with elected officials, policy makers and business leaders.

Small Business Development Centers (SBDC)

sba.gov/local-assistance/resource-partners/small-business-development-centers-sbdc

This is a nationwide network, often hosted by universities and colleges, that provides free, confidential business consulting and low-cost training to entrepreneurs and small business owners. Funded in part by the SBA, SBDCs offer a wide range of assistance from business plan development and financial management to marketing and access to capital, aiming to promote small business growth and contribute to the economy.

National Federation of Independent Businesses (NFIB)

NFIB.com

NFIB is a non-profit organization that serves as the voice of small and independent businesses in the United States. It advocates for the interests of its members, representing them in Washington, D.C. and all 50 state capitals. The organization provides resources, research and legal support to help small businesses thrive.

FINANCIAL, LEGAL AND TAX SUPPORT

100+ Grants, Loans, and Programs to Benefit Your Small Business

https://www.uschamber.com/co/run/business-financing/small-business-grants-and-programs

I was doing some research for an upcoming book on small business financing and landed on this little gem. It's a list of loans, small business grants and other financing opportunities that the U.S. Chamber of Commerce updates every week. Check it out.

FDIC: Money Smart for Small Business

Fdic.gov/consumer-resource-center/money-smart-small-business

Boost your financial literacy with 13 modules for starting and managing a business. The materials and instructor-led curriculum were developed jointly by the Small Business Administration and Federal Deposit Insurance Corporation (FDIC). You can download financial resources right from the catalog, which is online here.

IRS Small Business and Self-Employed Tax Center

Irs.gov/businesses/small-businesses-self-employed

Get answers to your small business tax questions at the IRS Small Business and Self-Employed Tax Center. It provides free resources for taxpayers who file Form 1040 or 1040-SR and small companies with assets under $10 million. Some of the key topics covered include tax prep, filing/paying taxes and the stages of business ownership.

Nav

Nav.com

Nav is a financial health platform for small businesses. It allows entrepreneurs to see potential financing options they may qualify for before applying. For instance, a business owner signs up for a free account and inputs business data (like credit history and bank transactions). Then, Nav compares your information against funding requirements from more than 200 partners.

Find Law

Findlaw.com

FindLaw is an online legal resource and a platform that business owners and others can use to connect with legal professionals. It offers a library of free, accessible legal information on various business topics, from choosing a business structure and intellectual property to contracts and tax obligations.

LegalZoom

Legalzoom.com

LegalZoom provides online legal solutions for small businesses and individuals, making it easier to form various business entities like LLCs and corporations, register trademarks and draft legal documents.

ZenBusiness

Zenbusiness.com

ZenBusiness offers streamlined services for forming LLCs, corporations and other business structures. Its goal is to simplify the legal and administrative steps involved in starting a business, including registered agent services, operating agreement templates and compliance assistance.

ACCOUNTING & FINANCIAL MANAGEMENT

QuickBooks

Quickbooks.com

QuickBooks is a widely used accounting software for small businesses. It helps manage income and expenses, track sales, process invoices and generate financial reports, making bookkeeping more efficient for entrepreneurs. There are various versions, depending on your needs, including desktop and cloud-based options.

Wave Accounting

Waveapps.com

Wave offers free accounting software for small businesses, including invoicing, expense tracking and financial reporting tools. The app is particularly popular with freelancers and very small businesses looking for an accessible way to manage their finances. It also offers paid services like payroll.

FreshBooks

Freshbooks.com

FreshBooks is cloud-based accounting software designed for small business owners and freelancers, particularly those in service-based industries. It simplifies financial management by offering tools for invoicing clients, tracking expenses and time, managing projects and generating financial reports.

MARKETING & WEB SOLUTIONS

Google My Business

business.google.com/us/business-profile/

Use this free tool to manage your online presence across Google, including both Search and Maps. It helps businesses appear in local search results, engage with customers through reviews and share important information like hours and contact details.

Canva

Canva.com

Canva is an online graphic design tool that helps entrepreneurs create professional-looking marketing materials without extensive design experience. It offers templates for social media posts, presentations, flyers, logos and more, making visual content creation accessible.

Mailchimp

Mailchimp.com

This all-in-one marketing platform helps small businesses manage email marketing campaigns, build landing pages, create websites and automate marketing efforts. It's a popular choice for building email lists and engaging with customers.

Squarespace

Squarespace.com

Another all-in-one platform, Squarespace helps companies build visually appealing websites, online stores and portfolios. It's known for its user-friendly interface and professionally designed templates, making it accessible for entrepreneurs to create a strong online presence without needing extensive technical skills. It also offers features like scheduling, email campaigns and analytics.

Hootsuite

Hootsuite.com

This social media management platform helps you manage and schedule posts across multiple social networks from a single dashboard. I've used it before to streamline my social media efforts, support my content creation, schedule posts, track performance and manage customer engagement all in one place.

Hubspot

Hubspot.com

Hubspot provides an integrated suite of tools designed to help small businesses grow by managing their marketing, sales, customer service and content. It centralizes customer data, automates marketing campaigns, helps manage sales pipelines and provides tools for customer support, website building and analytics.

Constant Contact

Constantcontact.com

This email marketing and automation platform was made for small businesses and non-profits. It provides user-friendly tools for creating professional email campaigns, managing contact lists, segmenting audiences and tracking performance. It also offers features for building websites, e- commerce stores, social media marketing and event management.

MOTIVATIONAL BUSINESS PODCASTS

Masters of Scale
Mastersofscale.com
Hosted by LinkedIn co-founder Reid Hoffman, this podcast explores theories of how companies grow from zero to a global scale. Each episode features Hoffman testing his theories against the experiences of legendary leaders, providing deep insights into scaling strategies, leadership, innovation and company culture, often with a focus on tech and rapid growth.

The Smart Passive Income Online Business and Blogging Podcast
Smartpassiveincome.com
For anyone interested in building online businesses and creating multiple income streams, Pat Flynn's podcast is a comprehensive resource. He shares practical strategies, case studies and interviews with experts on topics like online business models, passive income, digital marketing and leveraging personal brands, all with an emphasis on transparency and actionable advice.

The $100 MBA Show
100mba.net
This daily podcast offers concise, actionable business lessons designed to teach entrepreneurs everything they need to know about starting and running a business without the fluff. Omar Zenhom breaks down complex business concepts into bite-sized,

practical advice, covering a wide array of topics relevant to everyday entrepreneurial challenges and opportunities.

RECAP: 32 POWER TIPS IN ONE PLACE

Most of the chapters in this book concluded with a list of four action tips to get you started. Here are all 32 in one place so you can start using them right away:

1) **Write down what happens after someone buys from you.** Include confirmation, follow-up and how problems get handled so customers never fall into a black hole.

2) **Pick one customer you don't want to lose.** Watch how the relationship actually works. How often do you check in? How fast do you respond? Do they have to chase you down?

3) **Choose a single, basic standard and stick to it.** Decide how fast you'll respond or follow up and don't let that slide (even when things get busy).

4) **Use the churn gut check in the introduction as a starting point.** Any question you answer "no" to may already be a point where customers may be considering your competitors.

5) **Document what happens after your next sale.** Write down when customers hear from you again and who handles that follow-up.

6) **Identify one point where customers tend to drop off.** Look for gaps after delivery, onboarding or between repeat purchases.

7) **List the digital tools you already use to manage customers.** Include email, scheduling, CRM, invoicing or project tools and note what each one supports.

8) **Audit which retention tasks are automated versus manual.** Flag the areas where a simple trigger, template or reminder could prevent drop-off.

9) **Write down who your business is and isn't built for.** Be specific enough that you'd feel comfortable saying "no" to a prospect without questioning your decision.

10) **Envision your first five customers.** Focus on how they buy, what they value and why you're setting your sights on them.

11) **Check whether your pricing makes sense for the customers you want of.** If you're constantly explaining or defending it, something's off.

12) **Read your own marketing materials like you're seeing them for the first time.** Does the content speak to your ideal customer, or is it trying to be everything to everyone?

13) **Watch for early warning signs of churn.** Use the checklist in Chapter 4 to spot inconsistent service, slow responses and fading engagement.

14) **Map the first 30 days of a new client relationship.** Include onboarding, scheduling, communication, billing and follow-up.

15) **Standardize how service is delivered and explained.** Define what "good service" looks like so the experience feels familiar no matter who handles the work.

16) **Create a simple service punch list and use it for every client.** Document the key steps from first contact through follow-up so nothing gets skipped or handled differently.

17) **Pinpoint what happens after every order.** Write down the exact sequence from   confirmation to delivery to follow-up and fix the points where customers are left guessing or forgotten.

18) **Automate one post-delivery follow-up and make it non-negotiable.** Choose a single message that adds value after the order arrives and set it up to go out every time, without relying on memory or manual effort.

19) **Make repeat customers feel recognized without calling attention to it.** Use small signals like saved preferences, early access or tailored recommendations.

20) **Close the gaps where communication comes to a halt.** Look at where emails, messages or outreach drop off after the first sale and tighten those handoffs before customers slip away.

21) **Put real face time to good use.** Don't let the visit end without setting up what comes next, whether that's a return date, a reason to check back or a simple reminder.

22) **Turn the end of an interaction into a handoff, not a goodbye.** What you say or do in the final two minutes matters more than anything you post online or send out afterward.

23) **Let your POS system do some of the remembering for you.** When regulars don't have to reintroduce themselves every time, the experience feels easier and more personal without extra effort from staff.

24) **Fix the one moment customers see when you're under pressure.** Busy lines, rushed service or awkward wrap-ups can erode customer loyalty over time.

25) **Take inventory of recent clients.** List everyone you've worked with in the last 12–24 months and think about what it would take to start working with them again.

26) **Remove one barrier to reengagement.** Fix a process, handoff or habit that makes coming back to you harder than it needs to be.

27) **Strength your mid-project strategy.** Choose one habit from the punch list in Chapter 7 that you're not already doing and put it into action.

28) **End projects in a way that encourages continuation.** When you close out the work, make sure clients can easily picture working with you again (even if the timing isn't immediate).

29) **Get one process out of your head and onto paper or screen**. If it only exists in your memory, it won't hold up when things get busy.

30) **Follow through even when there's nothing to sell**. If customers only hear from you when you need something, they'll assume the relationship ends when the transaction closes.

31) **Build in a regular check for dormant customers.** Skip this step and you'll only notice customer churn after it's already happened.

32) **Capture customer context while it's fresh.** If you don't capture it in the moment, it may get watered down or lost altogether.

SHARE YOUR EXPERIENCE & HELP OTHERS START SMART

Starting a business isn't easy and I know firsthand how overwhelming it can feel. If *The Small Business Growth Blueprint* helped you plan, launch or grow your business, would you take a minute to share that in an Amazon review?

Your words can encourage the next entrepreneurs who are struggling to get their businesses to the next level and achieve their dreams. Reviews help others discover the book, see what's possible and take their first step.

Every review adds to a growing community of first-time business owners who are learning, building and succeeding together. I'd love for you to be part of it.

BUILD ON WHAT YOU'VE LEARNED

Keeping customers long-term starts with a business that's built to support them. *Your First Business Blueprint* helps you shape that foundation by guiding you through:

- Choosing a business with real revenue potential
- Turning an idea into a clear, workable plan
- Setting up your business and finances with confidence
- Putting simple systems in place that support consistency and growth

It's a practical guide for first-time founders who want to start smart and build something that lasts.

Clear planning makes it easier to build strong, lasting customer relationships. *Blueprints Beat Cocktail Napkins* gives you a practical way to think through the decisions that shape your business by helping you:

- Create a clear business plan using a proven step-by-step framework
- Define your market, pricing and financials with confidence
- Turn big-picture ideas into clear priorities and next steps
- Use planning tools that guide daily decisions and long-term growth
- Keep your plan relevant as your business evolves

This focused planning book includes digital tools that support the process and make it easier to apply what you've learned.

Both books are available on Amazon

ABOUT THE AUTHOR

First of all, much gratitude for allowing me to play a small role in your entrepreneurial journey. Know that I <u>do not</u> take that trust and responsibility lightly.

I'm Bridget McCrea. I've hustled through dead-end jobs, stretched a bank account that was almost empty, raised a toddler while chasing deadlines and built a business with nothing but determination, a desktop and a Texas Instruments 1200-baud modem at my kitchen table. For more than three decades I've been telling the real stories of entrepreneurs who took the same unpredictable path.

Three things I love most about being an entrepreneur & writer:

1) **Building something out of scraps.** I started with little more than grit, a toddler on my hip and a nearly empty bank account. I turned it into a business that lasted.

2) **Getting a front-row seat to other people's journeys.** From sitting across the table from inspiring female leaders like Mindy Grossman to hearing how R.W. Garcia's founders came up with the idea for tortilla salad strips, I've seen firsthand what it really takes to create something that lasts.

3) **Turning lessons into tools that help others.** Whether it's writing small business books, crafting a Dummies guide for Wiley or developing content for well-known companies like Toyota, Panasonic and SAP, I love distilling hard-won insights into something others can actually use.

I've written for major media outlets, picked up a few awards along the way and published books that people still keep on their shelves, including *Your First Business Blueprint* for first-time founders and *Blueprints Beat Cocktail Napkins* for business planning. Through it all, the real win is seeing readers like you put the lessons to work. If *The Small Business Growth Blueprint* helps you take even one solid step toward getting your company to the next level, then it's done its job.

RESOURCES

Here's a selection of key references and resources that I leaned on when writing this book. They're organized by chapter and all URLs were current and working as of January 2026.

Introduction

Gallo, Amy, The Value of Keeping the Right Customers, HBR
https://hbr.org/2014/10/the-value-of-keeping-the-right-customers

Frederick Reichheld of Bain & Company
www.bain.com/Images/BB_Prescription_cutting_costs.pdf

The 360 Blog, Top Customer Retention Tactics For Small Businesses and Startups, Salesforce
www.salesforce.com/blog/customer-retention-tips-for-small-business/

Chapter 2

Walmart vs. Target: An Analytical Comparison of Two American Retail Giants, MMCG Invest
www.mmcginvest.com/post/walmart-vs-target-an-analytical-comparison-of-two-american-retail-giants

Chapter 3

Salomon, Ben, Cost of Customer Acquisition vs. Retention: Stats & Strategy, Yotpo
www.yotpo.com/blog/cost-of-customer-acquisition-vs-retention

Bennett, Nicole, Average Customer Acquisition Cost by Industry: Tracking CAC Benchmarks, Vena Solutions
www.venasolutions.com/blog/average-cac-by-industry

9 digital marketing strategies for small businesses, Bank of America
https://business.bankofamerica.com/en/resources/digital-marketing-for-small-business

Luck, Ian, 5 Innovative Customer Retention Examples and Case Studies, CustomerGauge
https://customergauge.com/blog/customer-retention-examples

Chapter 5

Quarterly Retail E-Commerce Sales, US Census Bureau
www.census.gov/retail/ecommerce.html

Lebow, Sara, Ecommerce to account for more than 20% of worldwide retail sales despite slowdown, EMARKETER
www.emarketer.com/content/ecommerce-account-more-than-20--of-worldwide-retail-sales-despite-slowdown

The best customer retention strategies for e-commerce companies, Funnel.io
https://funnel.io/blog/customer-retention-e-commerce

14 Customer Retention Strategies That Help Increase ROI, Shopify
www.shopify.com/blog/customer-retention-strategies

Santora, Jacinda, How to Improve Ecommerce Customer Retention (5 Easy Ways), Help Scout
www.helpscout.com/blog/ecommerce-retention-marketing/

Chapter 6

Chatterjee, Sharmila C., The future of physical retail: 5 actions to elevate customer experience, MIT Management Sloan School
https://mitsloan.mit.edu/ideas-made-to-matter/future-physical-retail-5-actions-to-elevate-customer-experience

Chapter 7

Client Retention - How To Keep Your Freelance Clients Happy, ThriveThemes
https://thrivethemes.com/freelance-digital-marketing/client-retention

6 Ways to Deliver Better Customer Service as an Independent Contractor, Work for Impact
https://community.workforimpact.com/c/freelancer-tips/6-ways-to-deliver-better-customer-service-as-a-freelancer

MORE FROM THE STRONGTIDE PRESS LIBRARY

Your First Business Blueprint:
How to Plan, Launch and Grow a Profitable Small Business

Blueprints Beat Cocktail Napkins:
How to Create a Winning Business Plan for Growth and Profit

The Business Money Blueprint:
How to Find Funding, Close the Deal and Act on Your Plan

The Real Estate Agent's Business Planner:
The Proven System for Generating Leads,
Winning Clients and Building a Profitable Real Estate Career

The Real Estate Agent's 12-Month Planning Workbook:
The Month-by-Month Planner for Managing Leads, Clients, Income,
and Results